OH, GUS!

by orlando busino

ACKNOWLEDGMENTS

The cartoons in this book appeared originally in BOYS' LIFE, published by the Boy Scouts of America, and were copyrighted c in 1970, 1971, 1972, 1973, 1974, 1975, 1976, 1977, 1978, 1979, 1980, and 1981 by BOYS' LIFE.

Copyright © 1981 by Orlando Busino
ISBN 0-89319-016-0

ANDOR PUBLISHING, INC.
163 East Union Avenue
East Rutherford, N.J. 07073

"I'm sure I saw him wink at the owner when you agreed to the price."

"There are some things dogs don't do!
Climbing ladders is one of them."

"We'd all like to use the portable pool!"

"Now you're too far away, Gus ... step closer."

"Other dogs don't get tired when they walk with their masters!"

"That was a nice bark, Gus, but I don't think he knew you were just saying 'Hi'."

"These aren't mine, Gus! Quick, take them back to where you got them!"

"He swallowed my bird call — now when he tries to bark he whistles."

"Gus must have stopped chasing us and gone home — I don't see him anymore."

"I'll have you bathed in no time,
Gus — Gus? — Gus — ?"

"Relax, Gus, I'm only going to wash the car."

"I'm sorry you ever won that ribbon in the dog show!"

"I'm afraid he thinks this is a doggie bag."

"You sure have a weird sense of humor—now will you go back and bring my slippers?"

"Funny — 'bowwow' isn't here!"

"Relax — I'll let you know when I get to the article on the pet show."

"Watch the expression on the mailman's face when Gus says, 'Hello'."

"Does this mean Gus can't go with us?"

"Gus! Are you sitting on the mailman?"

"Oh, no! You've gone off your diet again!"

"When I put this summer uniform on, I knew this would happen — I just knew it."

"This is the wrong room, Gus—the obedience class is down the hall!"

"You've sure got a bad case of hiccups, Gus."

"He dives fancy — but he can only swim the dog paddle."

"Time for your walk, Gus."

"Relax, Gus! He just yelled 'bat,' not 'bath.'"

"This is the part I hate about giving Gus a bath."

"He always does that when I read a joke about mailmen."

"Thanks, Gus, but I think I can handle things myself."

"Roll over, Gus! Your snoring is keeping the whole neighborhood awake."

"If I've said it once, I've said it a hundred times —
'Gus, don't sit on my skateboard!' "

"Oh good! We're in time for the game — they're still playing the national anthem."

"Thanks!"

"Now do you know why I didn't want you to lean against the door?"

"C'mon, Gus! Relax and act natural!"

"Very funny! Now put Herman's dog house back where you found it."

"Relax! Once it's in your plate, nobody's going to know what it is."

"That's my chair!"

"Wasn't that Mr. Schultz, our mailman?"

"That's not what I meant when I said, 'Stay home.'"

"OK, that does it! Tomorrow you go on a diet!"

"No! No! You're supposed to fetch the ball!"

"Gus likes to be rocked to sleep."

"Yes, I lost a small transistor radio . . . er . . . Why?"

"It's always the same story — that dog runs after us ... we forget he's friendly and run ... we all gain momentum ... we stop ... he can't ... POW! ... so keep running!"

"I knew it was a mistake to put those skates on Gus!"

"Maybe we'd better pass him up. Our left rear tire isn't in very good shape."

"I hate to admit it, Gus, but you've got fleas."

"Well, it's back to obedience school for you!"

"Say, Gus, how'd you like to run around the yard for a while?"

"Cut it out, Gus! You can't win 'em all."

"I just spotted some inhabitants of this planet! They were covered with hair, had tails and looked like large dogs — Ugh! it was horrible!"

"Of course it's Gus! It's just that I gave him a bath and now he has the 'frizzies.'"

"Hey! What happened to my super-magnet?"

"Would you please go home and let us get some sleep?"

"Gus? . . . Oh, Gus? . . . Gus? . . ."

"I'm glad Gus is around when they show spooky pictures like this!"

"Did you jump up on poor Uncle Jasper's lap again, Gus?"

"Just bring them, Gus!"

"You weren't exactly a smashing success at the kite meet."

"How's that for reveille, Gus?"

"Hello, Mr. Stubbs — we're back again!"

"Too much TV."

"Oh, Gus! Wake up! Gus! Wake up! . . . ."

"I think our mailman is talking about you again, Gus."

"Gus should have been named 'Dinner.' It's the one word that really gets him to come."

"Now let me tell you the symptoms of another illness that might be troubling your pet . . ."

"... Joey? Tommy? Bobby? Gary? Jimmy? Harvey? ..."

"After the friendly way Gus greeted you, how can you help but like him?"

"I could have sworn I heard one of them bark."

"I don't think he wanted you to bark into his stethoscope, Gus."

"Do you have to act so weird everytime I play my portable radio?"

"I hope you weren't bothering the plumber again, Gus."

"Hundreds of normal dogs in this town — and I have to have a comedian on my route!"

"Relax, Gus."

"Separate checks."

"Hold it, Gus!"

"For a friendly dog, there are times when Gus can get on anybody's nerves."

"His exercise program should be over soon."

"...And this, junior scientist, is a picture of a flea, blown up a thousand times larger than life."

"There's one dog on this route you'll have trouble with. He doesn't bite but OH BROTHER!"

"Guess what, Gus? Mom says you can stay in tonight — even gave me a blanket for you to sleep on!"

"See, Gus? I told you not to follow us."

"You're supposed to BRING the slippers TO ME!"

"This isn't quite what I had in mind, Gus."

"Gus! What have you done now?"

"...Slowly a hairy hand moved toward our hero ..."

"... a new dog collar ... a box of dog biscuits ... a rubber bone ..."

"OK! What happened to my 10 pieces of bubble gum?"

"Gesundheit, and thanks a lot, Gus!"

"From now on, Gus, let me answer the phone."

"This is Gus. He discovered the short."

"From now on, no more extra snacks for Gus."

"Okay, Gus, what did you do with the soap?"

"We've got to warn people about Gus — this is the third time today he's accidentally stepped on someone's toes."

"Come on, Gus — this diet isn't going to be that bad."

"Try to keep Gus from eating too fast from now on."

"Help!"

"Next time, Gus, warn us before you jump in."

"I wasn't talking about food when
I said Gus doesn't bite."

THE AUTHOR

Orlando Busino decided he wanted to be a cartoonist when he was a nine year old boy growing up in Binghamton, N.Y.

Immediately after graduating from the State University of Iowa, Orlando attended the School of Visual Arts (known then as The Cartoonists and Illustrators School). He sold his first magazine cartoon to the old SATURDAY EVENING POST and has been a full time magazine cartoonist ever since. He has the rare distinction of having been selected by the National Cartoonist Society three times to receive The Best Magazine Cartoonist of the Year Award.

Besides drawing GUS for BOYS' LIFE, Orlando is a top contributor to LADIES HOME JOURNAL, GOOD HOUSEKEEPING, and other magazines. OH, GUS! is his second book, his first was GOOD BOY!, a collection of animal cartoons.

The cartoonist lives in Ridgefield, Ct. with his wife, children and pets.